COPYWORK
Genesis Curriculum

The Book of Matthew

First Edition

This workbook belongs to

_____

Welcome to the Genesis Curriculum Copywork. There is a verse a day to copy. The verse comes from the day's reading and is picked at times for practicing different things like semi-colon or quotation marks that are introduced in the curriculum. You can use the extra lines to have your child write their spelling words and sentences for the writing portion of the curriculum. The second page each day has the vocabulary word for the day. It gives the definition and example sentences. Then they can draw a picture to illustrate its meaning. They can use their own idea or use the example sentences for an idea of what to draw.

I've added this introduction page for another purpose as well. This will push back the first page so that their copying and vocabulary will be open on the same page. ☺

Have a great year learning together.

Day 1

Jesse was the father
of David the king.

_____

_____

_____

_____

_____

_____

_____

deportation

Color in today's vocabulary word. Draw a picture to show its meaning. It means sending someone out of a country by law. Here are some sentences that use the word.

The deportation of the Hebrews forced them from their homes in Israel.

Immigrants seek visas from the government to avoid deportation.

Day 2

And Joseph her husband, being a righteous man and not wanting to disgrace her, planned to send her away secretly.

_____

_____

_____

_____

_____

_____

_____

Color in today's vocabulary word. Draw a picture to show its meaning. It means innocent and inexperienced, or untouched. Here are some sentences that use the word.

The virgin forests are protected by the government to keep it untouched.

People knew he was a sailing virgin when he got sea sick.

Day 3

Gathering together all the chief priests and scribes of the people, he inquired of them where the Messiah was to be born.

_____

_____

_____

_____

_____

_____

_____

_____

determine

Color in today's vocabulary word. Draw a picture to show its meaning. It means to figure out in an exact fashion, to be the deciding factor. Here are some sentences that use the word.

We got out the map to determine exactly how much farther we needed to go.

Your attitude will determine how well you do your job.

Day 4

So Joseph got up, took the Child and His mother, and came into the land of Israel.

_____

_____

_____

_____

_____

_____

_____

Color in today's vocabulary word. Draw a picture to show its meaning. It means the surrounding area. Here are some sentences that use the word.

We decided to meet in the vicinity of the flower garden after the meeting.

Look all around in this vicinity; I'm sure I left it here.

Day 5

For a child will be born to us, a son will be given to us; And the government will rest on His shoulders; And His name will be called Wonderful Counselor, Mighty God, Eternal Father, Prince of Peace. Isaiah 9:6

_____

_____

_____

_____

_____

_____

_____

_____

belts

Make sure to draw the levers on a belt.

Day 6

But John tried to prevent Him, saying, "I have need to be baptized by You, and do You come to me?"

_____

_____

_____

_____

_____

_____

_____

_____

Color in today's vocabulary word. Draw a picture to show its meaning. It means to satisfy by drinking, or to put out a fire. Here are some sentences that use the word.

We went looking for a drinking fountain to quench our thirst.

We threw a blanket over the fire to quench it.

Day 7

Then Jesus was led up by the Spirit into the wilderness to be tempted by the devil.

_____

_____

_____

_____

_____

_____

_____

_____

Color in today's vocabulary word. Draw a picture to show its meaning. It means the highest point on a mountain or building, or the point of highest achievement. Here are some sentences that use the word.

The explorers reached the pinnacle of the mountain after years of effort in preparation and planning.

An Olympic gold medalist is at the pinnacle of their sport.

Day 8

From that time Jesus began to preach and say, "Repent, for the kingdom of heaven is at hand."

_____

_____

_____

_____

_____

_____

_____

_____

Color in today's vocabulary word. Draw a picture to show its meaning. It means to begin, to be understood, to start to become light. Here are some sentences that use the word.

It dawned on him that he was in the wrong place.

When she gave her life to Christ, she knew a whole new world had dawned.

Day 9

Jesus was going throughout all Galilee, teaching in their synagogues and proclaiming the gospel of the kingdom, and healing every kind of disease and every kind of sickness among the people.

_____

_____

_____

_____

_____

_____

_____

_____

Color in today's vocabulary word. Draw a picture to show its meaning. It means the state of not being able to function. Here are some sentences that use the word.

He was in a state of paralysis when he was called on to speak; he was so scared!

His paralysis made it so that he had to use a wheelchair to get around.

Day 10

Therefore if anyone is in Christ,
he is a new creature; the old things passed away;
behold, new things have come. 2 Corinthians 5:17

_____

_____

_____

_____

_____

_____

_____

_____

Colosseum

Draw a picture of the Colosseum.

Day 11

Let your light shine before men in such
a way that they may see your good works, and
glorify your Father who is in heaven.

_____

_____

_____

_____

_____

_____

_____

_____

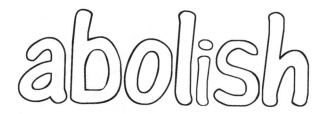

Color in today's vocabulary word. Draw a picture to show its meaning. It means to completely do away with something, or to annul and put an end to something by law. Here are some sentences that use the word.

The silly king abolished shoes from the kingdom, so everyone had to walk around barefoot.

I want to abolish complaining from my life.

Day 12

Truly I say to you, you will not come out
of there until you have paid up the last cent.

_____

_____

_____

_____

_____

_____

_____

_____

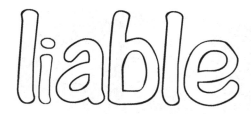

Color in today's vocabulary word. Draw a picture to show its meaning. It means to be declared responsible for something under the law, or to be likely to do something. Here are some sentences that use the word.

I am liable for the damages because I'm the one who broke their window.

He's liable to come through with the tickets we asked him to get for us.

Day 13

Nor shall you make an oath by your head, for you cannot make one hair white or black.

_____

_____

_____

_____

_____

_____

_____

_____

You can color in today's vocabulary word if you like. It means to give your body to someone who isn't your husband or wife. If you don't know what to draw, you can draw a picture of the right way, of a husband and wife being only for each other. Here are some sentences that use the word.

One of God's commandments is do not commit adultery.

God forgave the woman who committed adultery and told her to not sin anymore.

Day 14

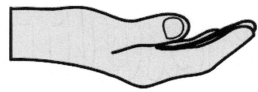

Give to him who asks of you, and do not turn away from him who wants to borrow from you.

_____

_____

_____

_____

_____

_____

_____

persecute

Color in today's vocabulary word. Draw a picture to show its meaning. It means to treat someone in a cruel way because of something about them, such as what they look like or what they believe. Here are some sentences that use the word.

The Pharisees persecuted Jesus to the point of having Him killed.

Some Roman emperors persecuted Christians, throwing them in prison, beating them, and even killing them.

Day 15

And you shall love the Lord your God with all your heart, and with all your soul, and with all your mind, and with all your strength. Mark 12:30

_____

_____

_____

_____

_____

_____

_____

perspective

We learned about perspective today. Can you draw a cube that looks like a block instead of looking flat?

Day 16

Beware of practicing your righteousness before men to be noticed by them; otherwise you have no reward with your Father who is in heaven.

_____

_____

_____

_____

_____

_____

_____

_____

Color in today's vocabulary word. Draw a picture to show its meaning. It means someone who acts opposite of what they say they believe. Here are some sentences that use the word.

He was a hypocrite when he told us we shouldn't have sugar and then went and drank a soda.

Jesus called the Pharisees hypocrites for teaching God's laws but not obeying them.

Day 17

For if you forgive others for their transgressions, your heavenly Father will also forgive you.

_____

_____

_____

_____

_____

_____

_____

transgressions

Color in today's vocabulary word. Draw a picture to show its meaning. It means to break the law. Here are some sentences that use the word.

Because Jesus died for us our sins can be forgiven.

His transgressions against the law will be held against them.

Day 18

Do not store up for yourselves treasures on earth, where moth and rust destroy, and where thieves break in and steal.

_____

_____

_____

_____

_____

_____

_____

_____

Color in today's vocabulary word. Draw a picture to show its meaning. It means to destroy, to put an end to something, to completely do away with it. Here are some sentences that use the word.

He eradicated the weeds from the garden.

God eradicated Sodom because of the sin of those in the city.

Day 19

But if your eye is bad, your
whole body will be full of darkness. If then the light
that is in you is darkness, how great is the darkness!

_____

_____

_____

_____

_____

_____

_____

_____

Color in today's vocabulary word. Draw a picture to show its meaning. It means to strongly dislike something or someone. Here are some sentences that use the word.

He despised dirt and turned his nose up at going on a picnic.

Don't despise those who are different from you.

Day 20

Our Father who is in heaven, hallowed be Your name. Your kingdom come. Your will be done, on earth as it is in heaven. Matthew 6:9-10

_____

_____

_____

_____

_____

_____

_____

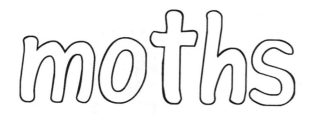

moths

Can you draw a picture that shows something or many things you learned about moths?

Day 21

So do not worry about tomorrow; for tomorrow will care for itself. Each day has enough trouble of its own.

_____

_____

_____

_____

_____

_____

_____

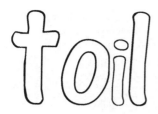

Color in today's vocabulary word. Draw a picture to show its meaning. It means to work long and hard at something, to work at something with a lot of effort. Here are some sentences that use the word.

He toiled long and hard to finish building the fence before night fall.

To spend your life toiling away only to get more and more money and things is not a wise way to live.

Day 22

Why do you look at the speck that is in your brother's eye, but do not notice the log that is in your own eye?

_____

_____

_____

_____

_____

_____

_____

_____

Color in today's vocabulary word. Draw a picture to show its meaning. It means to walk so heavily that you crush things under your feet or to treat something as worthless. Here are some sentences that use the word.

The boys trampled the flower garden as they chased each other playing tag.

Don't trample on her feelings by gloating over your victory.

Day 23

Ask, and it will be given to you; seek, and you will find; knock, and it will be opened to you.

_____

_____

_____

_____

_____

_____

_____

_____

devoted

Color in today's vocabulary word. Draw a picture to show its meaning. It means loyal, completely loving. Here are some sentences that use the word.

Her devoted dog followed her everywhere.

She was devoted to the idea of winning the science fair, so she worked day and night on her project.

Day 24

Beware of the false prophets, who come to you in sheep's clothing, but inwardly are ravenous wolves.

_____

_____

_____

_____

_____

_____

_____

ravenous

Color in today's vocabulary word. Draw a picture to show its meaning. It means very hungry, or eager or greedy for food or satisfaction. Here are some sentences that use the word.

The teenage boys were ravenous for dinner.

The bad guy was ravenous for revenge.

Day 25

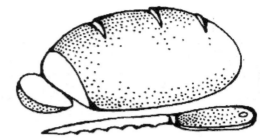

Give us this day our daily bread. And forgive us our debts, as we also have forgiven our debtors. And do not lead us into temptation, but deliver us from evil. Matthew 6:11-13

_____

_____

_____

_____

_____

_____

_____

_____

rain

Can you draw a picture of something you learned about today?

Day 26

Bop or Jump

Bounce a balloon or ball or jump over a jump rope or come up with another bop or jump idea. Every time the ball bounces or you jump over the rope, say the next letter in a word.

Here are some words for you to spell.

deportation   vicinity

treasure   shepherd

Day 27

Arts and Crafts Spelling

Write as many of these words as you can on a separate white piece of paper using a white crayon. Do your best. It's a little tricky! Then paint over your page with watercolor paint or just food coloring in water.

repentance

unquenchable

baptized

immediately

devil

pinnacle

minister

glory

region

beyond

shadow

dawned

synagogues

disease

various

crowd

Day 28

Ball Toss

Here are some words from our spelling list that you can use for the game. You can use this page to help you. Look at them carefully now. Think about each letter and what sounds the letters make in the words.

accomplished   vow

opponent   borrow

Day 29

Tic Tac Toe

Play tic-tac-toe. Draw a board. Decide who is X and who is O. Choose a square to play for. If you spell your word correctly, you can draw an X or O in the square. If you both choose the same square and both spell your word correctly, then leave the square blank.

Musical Chairs

You can play with your siblings on this game. Try to not be left standing. If you are, you'll have to spell a word, or part of a word. Here's a reminder for you.

WOLF becomes WOLVES and LILY becomes LILIES when they are made plural.

Day 31

BINGO

When you hear a definition, look to see if the word is on your board. If it is, place a marker over it.

When you have made a line of four words, call out BINGO!

devoted	despise	persecute	virgin
toil	abolish	quench	pinnacle
eradicate	vicinity	annul	paralysis
ravenous	trample	devoted	adultery

Day 32

Parts of Speech Sardines

You can play with your older siblings on this one, but you can also practice here.

Which word in each group of words is a noun, verb, or adjective? Circle it.

NOUN: throw   red   crown   passing

VERB: beautiful   tickle   ordinary   water

ADJECTIVE: grapes   cry   laugh   smooth

NOUN: pillow   green   ran   read

VERB: flowers   mild   friendly   bring

ADJECTIVE: grass   generous   ladybug   hop

Make a Sentence

Can you think of a sentence that would use one of these words?

- ▢   vicinity: the surrounding area

- ▢   quench: to satisfy by drinking, or to put out a fire

- ▢   pinnacle: the highest point, or the point of highest achievement

- ▢   dawn: to begin, to be understood, to start to become light

- ▢   trample: to walk so heavily that you crush things under your feet; to treat something as worthless

- ▢   devoted: loyal, completely loving

- ▢   ravenous: very hungry, or eager or greedy for food or satisfaction

_____

_____

Make a Sentence

Reorder the words and punctuation to fix the sentence.

my on nibble likes . funny to goat The coat

_____

_____

Day 35

Label the picture with at least three of your vocabulary words. You can add to the drawing if you feel you need to. You can see the vocabulary list from Day 33 for some words to consider.

Day 36

And they cried out, saying, "What business do we have with each other, Son of God? Have You come here to torment us before the time?"

_____

_____

_____

_____

_____

_____

_____

Color in today's vocabulary word. Draw a picture to show its meaning. It means to beg and ask for something in an emotional and very serious way. Here are some sentences that use the word.

The prisoner implored the judge to release him.

The woman implored Jesus to heal her daughter.

Day 37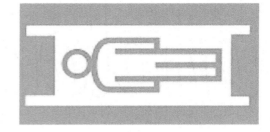

And they brought to Him a paralytic lying on a bed. Seeing their faith, Jesus said to the paralytic, "Take courage, son; your sins are forgiven."

_____

_____

_____

_____

_____

_____

_____

Color in today's vocabulary word. Draw a picture to show its meaning. It means filled with awe, a mixture of fear, respect, and wonder. Here are some sentences that use the word.

He was awestruck by the massive lightning storm.

I am awestruck when I think of God's power and love at work in the world.

Day 38

When the Pharisees saw this, they said to His disciples, "Why is your Teacher eating with the tax collectors and sinners?"

_____

_____

_____

_____

_____

_____

_____

_____

preserve

Color in today's vocabulary word. Draw a picture to show its meaning. It means preserve: to keep alive, to make last, to keep safe, to maintain, to keep in possession. Here are some sentences that use the word.

She wanted to preserve the memory, so she brought home a souvenir.

He wanted to preserve the wild flowers, so he was careful to mow around them.

Day 39

He said, "Leave; for the girl has not died, but is asleep." And they began laughing at Him.

_____

_____

_____

_____

_____

_____

_____

Color in today's vocabulary word. Draw a picture to show its meaning. It means outside edge. Here are some sentences that use the word.

The fringe on the rug keeps getting stuck in the vacuum cleaner.

She hung out on the fringe not knowing how to introduce herself to the strangers in the room.

Day 40

Jesus Christ is the same yesterday and today and forever. Hebrews 13:8

_____

_____

_____

_____

_____

_____

_____

_____

Newsies

What can you draw to show something you learned about the Newsies?

Day 41

Jesus summoned His twelve disciples and gave them authority over unclean spirits, to cast them out, and to heal every kind of disease and every kind of sickness.

_____

_____

_____

_____

_____

_____

_____

_____

dispirited

Color in today's vocabulary word. Draw a picture to show its meaning. It means discouraged, despondent. Here are some sentences that use the word.

The dispirited team climbed back onto the bus after their ten to nothing loss.

They became dispirited when the wall fell off the playhouse they had been trying to build.

Day 42

 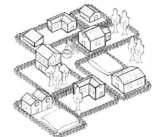

And whatever city or village you enter, inquire who is worthy in it, and stay at his house until you leave that city.

_____

_____

_____

_____

_____

_____

_____

_____

tolerable

Color in today's vocabulary word. Draw a picture to show its meaning. It means able to be tolerated, meaning you can stand it. Here are some sentences that use the word.

I found dinner barely tolerable but I said thank you anyway.

The noise level was just not tolerable to me, so I waited in the car for everyone else.

Day 43

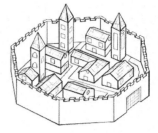

But whenever they persecute you in one city, flee to the next; for truly I say to you, you will not finish going through the cities of Israel until the Son of Man comes.

_____

_____

_____

_____

_____

_____

_____

Color in today's vocabulary word. Draw a picture to show its meaning. It means to meanly say bad things about another person in front of others. Here are some sentences that use the word.

The presidential candidates malign each other in the press.

It's wrong to spread rumors to malign another person.

Day 44

Are not two sparrows sold for a cent? And yet not one of them will fall to the ground apart from your Father.

_____

_____

_____

_____

_____

_____

_____

conceal

Color in today's vocabulary word. Draw a picture to show its meaning. It means to hide something, including keeping a secret. Here are some sentences that use the word.

She thought she had concealed the evidence that she had snuck a cookie, but her mom saw the crumbs.

Don't conceal the fact that you are struggling with a temptation. Tell someone about it. Satan wants you to keep things hidden in darkness. Bring it into the light because Jesus is the Light.

Day 45

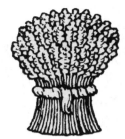

Then he said to his disciples, "The harvest is plentiful, but the laborers are few; therefore pray earnestly to the Lord of the harvest to send out laborers into his harvest." Matthew 9:37-38

_____

_____

_____

_____

_____

_____

_____

_____

refrigerator

Can you draw a picture about how refrigerators work?

Day 46

When Jesus had finished giving instructions to His twelve disciples, He departed from there to teach and preach in their cities.

_____

_____

_____

_____

_____

_____

_____

imprison

Color in today's vocabulary word. Draw a picture to show its meaning. It means to put in prison or to be trapped as if in prison. Here are some sentences that use the word.

The Christians were imprisoned for sharing their faith.

They were imprisoned by their fear and wouldn't venture out of their home.

Day 47

Truly I say to you, among those born of women there has not arisen anyone greater than John the Baptist! Yet the one who is least in the kingdom of heaven is greater than he.

_____

_____

_____

_____

_____

_____

_____

gluttonous

Color in today's vocabulary word. Draw a picture to show its meaning. It means someone who wants too much of something, especially food and drink. Here are some sentences that use the word.

The gluttonous king could barely walk on his own.

The gluttonous dog got into his treats and finished off the whole bag.

Day 48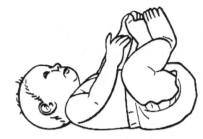

At that time Jesus said, "I praise You, Father, Lord of heaven and earth, that You have hidden these things from the wise and intelligent and have revealed them to infants."

_____

_____

_____

_____

_____

_____

_____

denounce

Color in today's vocabulary word. Draw a picture to show its meaning. It means to declare to others that someone or something is wrong or evil. Here are some sentences that use the word.

We denounce the involvement of the government in determining what churches can or cannot teach.

The president denounced the terrorists' actions.

Day 49

But when the Pharisees saw this, they said to Him, "Look, Your disciples do what is not lawful to do on a Sabbath."

_____

_____

_____

_____

_____

_____

_____

condemn

Color in today's vocabulary word. Draw a picture to show its meaning. It means to declare something wrong or no good for use, or to be forced into an unpleasant situation. Here are some sentences that use the word.

The building was condemned and a date was set for it to be demolished.

She condemned the use of alcohol among teenagers.

Day 50

Take My yoke upon you and learn from Me, for I am gentle and humble in heart, and you will find rest for your souls. For My yoke is easy and My burden is light. Matthew 11: 28 - 30

_____

_____

_____

_____

_____

_____

_____

withering plants

Draw a plant withering. Show the cause.

Day 51

All the crowds were amazed, and were saying, "This man cannot be the Son of David, can he?"

_____

_____

_____

_____

_____

_____

_____

_____

smoldering

Color in today's vocabulary word. Draw a picture to show its meaning. It means burning but with only smoke and no flames, or feeling strong emotion but not showing it. Here are some sentences that use the word.

Smoke from the smoldering fire was blowing in our faces.

He was smoldering over his loss and vowed to himself that next time he would win.

Day 52

If Satan casts out Satan, he is divided against himself; how then will his kingdom stand?

_____

_____

_____

_____

_____

_____

_____

blasphemy

Color in today's vocabulary word. Draw a picture to show its meaning. It means disrespectfully talking or acting toward God or sacred things. Here are some sentences that use the word.

Jesus was accused of blasphemy because He claimed to be God's son.

He considered it blasphemy for anyone to speak badly about Elvis' music.

Day 53

Then some of the scribes and Pharisees said to Him, "Teacher, we want to see a sign from You."

_____

_____

_____

_____

_____

_____

_____

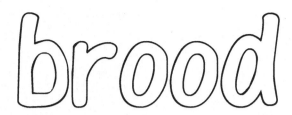

Color in today's vocabulary word. Draw a picture to show its meaning. It means a group, species, kind, especially a family's children; or it can mean to think over something insistently, especially something that's bothering you.

Here are some sentences that use the word.

The mother duckling ushered her brood in a parade through the park.

He brooded over her mistake instead of forgiving her.

Day 54

Someone said to Him, "Behold, Your mother and Your brothers are standing outside seeking to speak to You."

_____

_____

_____

_____

_____

_____

_____

unoccupied

Color in today's vocabulary word. Draw a picture to show its meaning. It means empty, no one living there; it could also mean no busy doing anything or a country that isn't being controlled by an invading army.

Since I was unoccupied, I volunteered to set the table.

The building was still unoccupied after it had been vacated more than a year ago.

Day 55

"Do not fear, for I am with you; do not anxiously look about you, for I am your God. I will strengthen you, surely I will help you, surely I will uphold you with My righteous right hand." Isaiah 41:10

_____

_____

_____

_____

_____

_____

_____

The Seven Seas

Can you draw a map of the "seven seas?" You can decide which ones to do.

Day 56

And the disciples came and said to Him, "Why do You speak to them in parables?"

_____

_____

_____

_____

_____

_____

_____

abundance

Color in today's vocabulary word. Draw a picture to show its meaning. It means more than enough. Here are some sentences that use the word.

After the harvest there was an abundance of food to share and enjoy.

An abundance of love is worth more than an abundance of money.

Day 57

And the one on whom seed was sown on the good soil, this is the man who hears the word and understands it; who indeed bears fruit and brings forth, some a hundredfold, some sixty, and some thirty.

_____

_____

_____

_____

_____

_____

_____

_____

Color in today's vocabulary word. Draw a picture to show its meaning. It means to grab suddenly. Here are some sentences that use the word.

He snatched the picture out of my hand to see what I was looking at.

The thief snatched the phone right out from under their noses.

Day 58

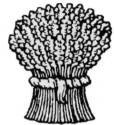

But while his men were sleeping, his enemy came and sowed tares among the wheat, and went away.

_____

_____

_____

_____

_____

_____

_____

_____

superior
inferior

Color in today's vocabulary words. Draw a picture to show their meanings. They mean something that's better and worse than expected. Here are some sentences that use the words.

He did a superior job painting the door, making it look brand new.

He did an inferior job painting the door, leaving drips everywhere.

Day 59

He spoke another parable to them, "The kingdom of heaven is like leaven, which a woman took and hid in three pecks of flour until it was all leavened."

_____

_____

_____

_____

_____

_____

_____

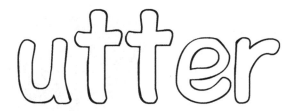

Color in today's vocabulary word. Draw a picture to show its meaning. It means to make a sound, or it can mean complete and total. Here are some sentences that use the word.

He uttered an unrecognizable syllable before running out of the room.

The children told a story that was utter nonsense, but they thought it was hysterical.

Day 60

"Do not store up for yourselves treasures on earth, where moth and rust destroy, and where thieves break in and steal. But store up for yourselves treasures in heaven...for where your treasure is, there your heart will be also."

_____

_____

_____

_____

_____

_____

_____

_____

economics

What can you draw that shows something you learned about economics?

Day 61

Color the whole page in lots of bright colors. Then color over the whole page in black crayon. Write spelling words on the page by writing with something that can scrape away the black top layer.

Here are some of your spelling words: steep, crossed, city, lying, collectors, healthy, unshrunk, follow, fringe, courage, noisy.

Day 62

Can you put these word parts together to make one word? You could cut them out and put them together or you could just write them on the line below.

____

LER

TO

ABLE

This page is left blank for the cutting activity on the previous page.

Day 63

Play the spelling race. Roll a die. If you roll a one, put a check in the first blank for number 1. Keep going until you have a winner. Write the "names" of the winners.

Finish Line!

1 priests ____ ____ ____ ____ ____

2 expected ____ ____ ____ ____ ____

3 messenger ____ ____ ____ ____ ____

4 prophesied ____ ____ ____ ____ ____

5 occurred ____ ____ ____ ____ ____

6 accept ____ ____ ____ ____ ____

First Place: _____   Second Place: _____

Third Place: _____   Fourth Place: _____

Day 64

Mother May I?

Play Mother May I with your older siblings. Listen to the sounds in the words and think about what letters make those sounds.

Day 65

Directions:

This is like the game Battleship. I set this up so that you can play with a sibling using the Genesis Curriculum Workbook.

Players write six words on their board, one letter per square. (I wrote in your words for you.) The words can go top to bottom and left to right. Words can intersect (share a letter, like in a crossword puzzle).

Players take turns guessing a square by naming its number and letter position. The other player must say either that it is blank or the letter in the square. If that square is blank, the player can place a dot or X in the square on the opponent's board to mark that it's been guessed already. If the square has a letter in it, the letter should be written in the square on the opponent's board.

You do not need to write on your board during the game. You just keep track of the game on the opponent's board. When you are asked about a square, you will check and tell what's in the square on the "My Ships" board.

The winner is the first to find all the letters of all six words on the opponent's board, in other words, to sink the opponent's word ships.

MY OPPONENT'S SHIPS

	1	2	3	4	5	6	7	8	9
A									
B									
C									
D									
E									
F									
G									
H									
I									

Day 60 words: parables, understand, prophecy, scarcely, sower, snatches, temporary, persecution, tares, enemy, gather, harvest, grown, leaven, foundation, utter

MY SHIPS

	1	2	3	4	5	6	7	8	9
A	E	U		T	A	R	E	S	
B	N	T							
C	E	T							
D	M	E			S	O	W	E	R
E	Y	R							
F									
G	P	A	R	A	B	L	E	S	
H				G	R	O	W	N	
I									

Day 66

Circle the letters that should be capitalized: the first letter in every sentence and all names. Cheerios is the name of a cereal. Monday is the name of a day of the week. Walmart is the name of a store.

please put these where they belong, sarah.

my birthday is on tuesday.

our cell phone company is verizon.

i love the book the little engine that could.

sabrina lives in germany.

Day 67

Charades! Act out the words. Use the list below to choose words and to help you guess words. I put some that I thought would be easier to act out up top.

implore: to beg and ask for something in an emotional and very serious way

awestruck: filled with awe, which is a mixture of fear, respect, and wonder

snatch: to grab suddenly

conceal: to hide something, including keeping a secret

imprison: to put in prison or to be trapped as if in prison

fringe: outside edge

dispirited: discouraged, despondent

tolerable: able to be tolerated, meaning you can stand it

malign: to meanly say bad things about another person in front of others

gluttonous: someone who wants too much of something, especially food and drink

denounce: to declare to others that someone or something is wrong or evil

condemn: to declare something wrong or no good for use, or to be forced into an unpleasant situation

smoldering: burning but with only smoke and no flames, feeling strong emotion but not show it

blasphemy: disrespectfully talking or acting toward God or sacred things

brood: a group, species, kind, especially a family's children (noun), to think over something insistently, especially something that's bothering you (verb)

unoccupied: vacant, deserted, abandoned, empty, no one living there

preserve: to keep alive, to make last, to keep safe, to maintain, or to keep in possession

abundance: more than enough

superior and inferior: good/bad, when something is better or worse than expected

utter: to make a sound or to say something; total, complete

Day 68

Go on a picnic. You can play this with your older siblings, but you can do a little here as well. Fill in the blanks with a word of the correct part of speech that starts with the same letter of the alphabet of the other words on the line.

I saw a/an...

adventurous _____ acting atrociously
                     noun

brainy bear _____ barbarically
                     verb

_____ cat coughing catastrophically
    adjective

Day 69

The words in this paragraph have been all mixed up! Can you put them back in the right place?

After our <u>abundance</u> appetite was satisfied, we walked to the lake. We were <u>ravenous</u> at the sight of the sun reflecting off the lake. There is an <u>awestruck</u> of beauty in nature. I decided that was enough of standing still, but I <u>snatched</u> my plan until I suddenly <u>concealed</u> my brother's hand and pulled him into the water with me.

After our _____ appetite was satisfied,

we walked to the lake. We were _____

at the sight of the sun reflecting off the lake. There

is an _____ of beauty in nature. I

decided that was enough of standing still, but I

_____ my plan until I suddenly

_____ my brother's hand and pulled

him into the water with me.

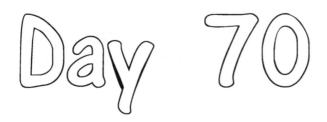

Treasure hunt! Write a treasure hunt using verbs, nouns, and adjectives to describe where the others should look to find the treasure and how they should get there. Should they crawl under the black table and look beside the red cabinet?

_____

_____

_____

_____

Day 71

Six days later Jesus took with Him Peter and James and John his brother, and led them up on a high mountain by themselves.

_____

_____

_____

_____

_____

_____

_____

timorous

Color in today's vocabulary word. Draw a picture to show its meaning. It means full of fear. Here are some sentences that use the word.

He felt timorous walking around the dark room after the lights went out.

We don't have to be timorous in sharing our faith because God will give us the words to say.

Day 72

As they were coming down from the mountain, Jesus commanded them, saying, "Tell the vision to no one until the Son of Man has risen from the dead."

_____

_____

_____

_____

_____

_____

_____

_____

Color in today's vocabulary word. Draw a picture to show its meaning. It means rejuvenate, renew, revive, repair, renovate, or bring back. Here are some sentences that use the word.

They bought an old historic home hoping to restore it.

He asked his friend for forgiveness hoping to restore their friendship.

Day 73

Then the disciples came to Jesus privately and said, "Why could we not drive it out?"

_____

_____

_____

_____

_____

_____

_____

_____

Color in today's vocabulary word. Draw a picture to show its meaning. It means free from a requirement. Here are some sentences that use the word.

I'm hoping to get exempt from my work today since I'm not feeling well.

No one should be exempt from obeying the law.

Day 74

At that time the disciples came to Jesus and said, "Who then is greatest in the kingdom of heaven?"

_____

_____

_____

_____

_____

_____

_____

converted

Color in today's vocabulary word. Draw a picture to show its meaning. It means changed from one character, form, or function to another. Here are some sentences that use the word.

After a tasty meal, she was converted from being a liver hater.

My first family home was a garage that had been converted into a little house.

Day 75

Finally, brethren, whatever is true, whatever is honorable, whatever is right, whatever is pure, whatever is lovely, whatever is of good repute, if there is any excellence and if anything worthy of praise, dwell on these things. Philippians 4:8

_____

_____

_____

_____

_____

_____

_____

Native Americans

Draw something you learned about Native Americans.

Day 76

"If your brother sins, go and show him his fault in private; if he listens to you, you have won your brother."

_____

_____

_____

_____

_____

_____

_____

_____

Color in today's vocabulary word. Draw a picture to show its meaning. It means to establish that something is correct. Here are some sentences that use the word.

I called to confirm that our flight is on time.

I Googled the fact to confirm it was correct.

Day 77

Then Peter came and said to Him, "Lord, how often shall my brother sin against me and I forgive him? Up to seven times?"

_____

_____

_____

_____

_____

_____

_____

_____

indolence

Color in today's vocabulary word. Draw a picture to show its meaning. It means laziness, decision to not endure. Here are some sentences that use the word.

I couldn't believe his indolence in just sitting there while I did all the work.

I couldn't give into indolence and give up instead of finishing the race, even though it was so hard.

Day 78

And his lord, moved with anger, handed him over to the torturers until he should repay all that was owed him.

_____

_____

_____

_____

_____

_____

_____

summon

Color in today's vocabulary word. Draw a picture to show its meaning. It means to demand someone come. Here are some sentences that use the word.

I got summoned to jury duty.

I think I'm in trouble. My mom just summoned me to come talk to her.

Day 79

Then some children were brought to Him so that He might lay His hands on them and pray; and the disciples rebuked them.

_____

_____

_____

_____

_____

_____

_____

_____

Color in today's vocabulary word. Draw a picture to show its meaning. It means agree to something, permit it. Here are some sentences that use the word.

He acceded to coming along.

I said, "Pretty please," until she acceded to my request for ice cream.

Day 80

Jesus said, "Let the little children come to me, and do not hinder them, for the kingdom of heaven belongs to such as these." Matthew 19:14

_____

_____

_____

_____

_____

_____

_____

_____

mitochondria

Make a drawing of characters that are mitochondria doing their job helping make energy for the cells.

Day 81

They said to him, "Because no one hired us." He said to them, "You go into the vineyard too."

_____

_____

_____

_____

_____

_____

_____

Color in today's vocabulary word. Draw a picture to show its meaning. It means not doing anything. Here are some sentences that use the word.

We were idle all afternoon since it just seemed too hot to work.

The sewing machine sat idle after the foot broke and never got replaced.

Day 82

Take what is yours and go, but I wish to give to this last man the same as to you.

_____

_____

_____

_____

_____

_____

_____

_____

envious

scorch

Color in today's vocabulary words. Draw pictures to show their meaning. They mean jealous and to burn. Here are some sentences that use the words.

You should be grateful for what you have instead of envious of what others have.

The pot holder was scorched where it had touched the flame.

Day 83

Then the mother of the sons of Zebedee came to Jesus with her sons, bowing down and making a request of Him.

_____

_____

_____

_____

_____

_____

_____

Color in today's vocabulary word. Draw a picture to show its meaning. It means to go on for a long time, or to put up with something, or to not give up when it's hard. Here are some sentences that use the word.

We endured the ten-mile hike even though it lasted for hours.

Several prisoners of the Nazis testify that their faith in Jesus enabled them to endure their suffering.

Day 84

As they were leaving Jericho, a large crowd followed Him.

_____

_____

_____

_____

_____

_____

_____

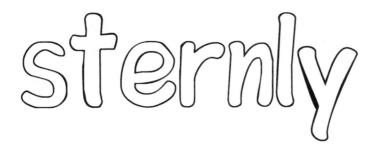

Color in today's vocabulary word. Draw a picture to show its meaning. It means strictly, firmly. Here are some sentences that use the word.

She sternly warned them to not go into the water when the surf was rough.

Their father spoke sternly to them after they hurt their brother because they were being wild.

Day 85

Be kind and compassionate to one another, forgiving each other, just as in Christ God forgave you. Ephesians 4:32

_____

_____

_____

_____

_____

_____

_____

baby animals

Can you draw and name some baby animals?

Day 86

Now in the morning, when He was returning to the city, He became hungry.

_____

_____

_____

_____

_____

_____

_____

indignant

Color in today's vocabulary word. Draw a picture to show its meaning. It means being upset over something you think is unfair. Here are some sentences that use the word.

She was indignant that she was told she was too young to play.

He was indignant when he read that in Macedonia most Roma children don't have the chance to go even to high school.

Day 87

Seeing this, the disciples were amazed and asked, "How did the fig tree wither all at once?"

_____

_____

_____

_____

_____

_____

_____

flabbergasted

Color in today's vocabulary word. Draw a picture to show its meaning. It means amazed, astounded, dumbfounded, astonished, staggered, surprised, awestruck. Here are some sentences that use the word.

I was flabbergasted by how much it cost.

We were flabbergasted when a whale came out of the water just next to us.

Day 88

When the harvest time approached, he sent his slaves to the vine-growers to receive his produce.

_____

_____

_____

_____

_____

_____

_____

_____

remorse

Color in today's vocabulary word. Draw a picture to show its meaning. It means a feeling of regret, of feeling really bad over something you've done wrong. Here are some sentences that use the word.

He showed remorse for having gotten angry.

She said she was sorry and truly showed remorse.

Day 89

When the chief priests and the Pharisees heard His parables, they understood that He was speaking about them.

_____

_____

_____

_____

_____

_____

_____

Color in today's vocabulary word. Draw a picture to show its meaning. It means very unhappy, unpleasant, bad, low quality. Here are some sentences that use the word.

What a wretched place this is! It smells like a trash dump.

Scrooge is a classic example of a wretched man.

Day 90

O LORD, You are my God; I will exalt You, I will give thanks to Your name; for You have worked wonders, plans formed long ago, with perfect faithfulness. Isaiah 25:1

_____

_____

_____

_____

_____

_____

_____

Chicago Fire

Draw a picture of people rebuilding or helping others after the fire.

Day 91

Those slaves went out into the streets and gathered together all they found, both evil and good; and the wedding hall was filled with dinner guests.

_____

_____

_____

_____

_____

_____

_____

_____

Color in today's vocabulary word. Draw a picture to show its meaning. It means to bite or grind your teeth together as an expression of anger or pain. Here are some sentences that use the word.

The prisoners gnashed their teeth when they heard they were not going to be released.

The bear gnashed his teeth when was caught in a trap.

Day 92

Tell us then, what do You think? Is it lawful to give a poll-tax to Caesar, or not?

_____

_____

_____

_____

_____

_____

_____

_____

Color in today's vocabulary word. Draw a picture to show its meaning. It means evil intentions, the desire to hurt or cause trouble for someone else. Here are some sentences that use the word.

You should never hold malice in your heart.

The Pharisees had malice toward Jesus.

Day 93

When the crowds heard this, they were astonished at His teaching.

_____

_____

_____

_____

_____

_____

_____

Color in today's vocabulary word. Draw a picture to show its meaning. It means to question, especially formally or in asking for information the person doesn't want to share. Here are some sentences that use the word.

My brother interrogated me when his soccer ball went missing.

Police interrogate suspects to try to figure out what happened.

Day 94

No one was able to answer Him a word, nor did anyone dare from that day on to ask Him another question.

_____

_____

_____

_____

_____

_____

_____

_____

preeminent

Color in today's vocabulary word. Draw a picture to show its meaning. It means superior, above others. Here are some sentences that use the word.

The pope is considered preeminent in the Catholic church.

Love is preeminent among the gifts and commands of God.

Day 95

And looking at them Jesus said to them, "With people this is impossible, but with God all things are possible." Matthew 19:26

_____

_____

_____

_____

_____

_____

_____

gravity

Diagram a picture of gravity in action.

Paper Chains

Write a letter on each strip and hook them together. Here are the words you'll be using.

eleventh, hour, idle, place, beginning, equal, envious, generous, scourge, raised, request, prepared, ransom, sternly, regain, mercy

Crossword

Fill the letters in the boxes to write the words in the puzzle. Use the length of the words and the letters already there give you the clues you need.

- question
- silenced
- invited
- plotted
- dead
- next

Fill in the Blank

Fill in the blanks with the letter pairs provided.

EE   OO   AU   IE   EA

l____se

agr____

rel____sed

pat____nce

f____lt

Day 99

Play Freeze Tag or Dungeon Escape

Here are the words you'll be playing with.

buying, house, robbers' den, withered, seeing,

amazed, doubt, source, afterwards, remorse,

landowner, larger, respect, wretched, proceed,

rejected

Word Search

Find as many spelling words as you can in the puzzle below. The words are up and down and forward across.

```
K  Z  T  E  R  R  I  F  I  E  D  X
I  T  B  X  P  C  F  M  G  E  D  U
R  J  E  E  R  D  W  S  G  K  G  N
E  C  X  M  I  R  H  I  R  B  U  B
C  M  C  P  V  O  I  X  E  K  C  E
O  C  E  T  A  W  T  G  A  J  U  L
G  A  P  V  T  N  E  V  T  A  S  I
N  U  T  J  E  E  C  P  E  C  T  E
I  S  G  Y  L  D  U  O  S  C  O  V
Z  E  K  X  Y  P  R  N  T  E  M  I
E  S  D  A  T  M  E  C  F  P  S  N
K  E  L  R  S  W  D  E  P  T  H  G
```

white, terrified, six, recognize, unbelieving, cured, once, privately, customs, except, accept, exempt, greatest, causes, drowned, depth

Vocabulary Review

Use this list as you review your vocabulary today.

timorous: full of fear (adjective)
restore: rejuvenate, renew, revive, repair, renovate, bring back (verb)
exempt: free from a requirement (adjective)
converted: changed from one character, form, or function to another (adjective)
confirm: to establish that something is correct, affirm, corroborate, substantiate (verb)
indolence: laziness, decision to not keep going (noun, indolent is the adjective)
summon: to demand someone come (verb)
accede: agree to something, permit it (verb)
idle: not doing anything (adjective)
envious: jealous (adjective)
scorch: to burn (verb)
endure: to go on for a long time, or to put up with something, or to not give up when it's hard (verb)
sternly: strictly, firmly (adverb)
indignant: being upset over something you think is unfair (adjective)
flabbergasted: amazed, astounded, dumbfounded, astonished, staggered, surprised, awestruck (adjective)
remorse: a feeling of regret, of feeling really bad over something you've done wrong (noun)
wretched: very unhappy, unpleasant, bad, low quality (adjective)
gnash: to bite or grind your teeth together as an expression of anger or pain (verb)
malice: evil intentions, the desire to hurt or cause trouble for someone else (noun)
interrogate: to question, especially formally or in asking for information the person doesn't want to share (verb)
preeminent: superior, above others (adjective)

Day 102

Grammar Review

Which is which? Draw lines to match the words to their parts of speech.

friend   happy   green   books   children

NOUN   VERB   ADJECTIVE

think   gravy   find   quiet   kick

Vocabulary Review

Match the words and their definitions.

timorous   repair, renew

restore   not doing anything

idle   full of fear

envious   to burn

scorch   jealous

endure   strictly

sternly   to not give up when it's hard

Writing Review

Think up as many alliterations as you can.

Here are some alliterations: Mickey Mouse, ticklish toddler, happy helper

_____

_____

_____

_____

_____

_____

Tell a Story

If you want to tell a big story with your siblings, use your Day 101 page for your vocabulary words. Otherwise, you can make up your own story about someone who was <u>timorous</u>, full of fear, or someone who was <u>indolent</u>, lazy. You can write it or just tell it to someone.

_____

_____

_____

_____

_____

_____

Day 106

For nation will rise against nation, and kingdom against kingdom, and in various places there will be famines and earthquakes.

_____

_____

_____

_____

_____

_____

_____

_____

tribulation

Color in today's vocabulary word. Draw a picture to show its meaning. It means pain and suffering or the cause of pain and suffering. Here are some sentences that use the word.

Jesus tells believers to expect tribulation.

Our family has held strong to our faith through all our tribulations.

Day 107

Whoever is on the housetop must not go down to get the things out that are in his house.

_____

_____

_____

_____

_____

_____

_____

_____

desolation

Color in today's vocabulary word. Draw a picture to show its meaning. It means complete emptiness of a place or a heart or the destruction of a place so completely that it becomes empty because it is uninhabitable. Here are some sentences that use the word.

The desolation after the tornado was heartbreaking.

The desolation in her heart after her mother died could only be filled by the love of Christ.

Day 108

For just as the lightning comes from the east and flashes even to the west, so will the coming of the Son of Man be.

_____

_____

_____

_____

_____

_____

_____

_____

Color in today's vocabulary word. Draw a picture to show its meaning. It means chosen person/people, or specifically chosen. Here are some sentences that use the word.

The elect are God's chosen people.

An elect group of people led us.

Day 109

Then there will be two men in the field; one will be taken and one will be left.

_____

_____

_____

_____

_____

_____

_____

_____

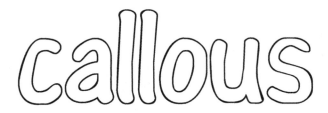

Color in today's vocabulary word. Draw a picture to show its meaning. It means uncaring, rough and tough. Here are some sentences that use the word.

His hands were callous after all his years working with wood.

His callous heart kept him from caring about anyone.

Day 110

He who testifies to these things says, "Yes, I am coming quickly." Amen. Come, Lord Jesus. The grace of the Lord Jesus be with all. Amen. Revelation 22:20-21

_____

_____

_____

_____

_____

_____

_____

Can you draw a picture of the planets having day and night or a diagram that shows why it's either day or night on a planet?

Day 111

Now while the bridegroom was delaying, they all got drowsy and began to sleep.

_____

_____

_____

_____

_____

_____

_____

_____

Color in today's vocabulary word. Draw a picture to show its meaning. It means making decisions carefully and wisely. Here are some sentences that use the word.

A prudent person seeks counsel from someone older and wiser.

It's good to be prudent when making decisions about spending money.

Day 112

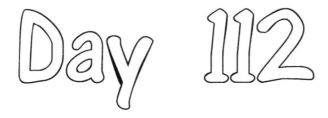

Immediately the one who had received the five talents went and traded with them, and gained five more talents.

_____

_____

_____

_____

_____

_____

_____

_____

Color in today's vocabulary word. Draw a picture to show its meaning. It means having no skill, clumsy. Here are some sentences that use the word.

He was inept at trying to follow the directions to build the furniture.

I felt inept trying to play along with the bell choir.

.

Day 113

Then you ought to have put my money in the bank, and on my arrival I would have received my money back with interest.

_____

_____

_____

_____

_____

_____

_____

Color in today's vocabulary word. Draw a picture to show its meaning. It means abundance or an excessive amount, more than needed. Here are some sentences that use the word.

We had a plethora of boxes after moving to our new home.

There is a plethora of choices at American stores.

Day 114

When did we see You sick, or in prison, and come to You?

_____

_____

_____

_____

_____

_____

_____

_____

Color in today's vocabulary word. Draw a picture to show its meaning. It means the amount to which something reaches. Here are some sentences that use the word.

We didn't know the extent of the damage caused by the storm.

To what extent do you think we'll need to be prepared?

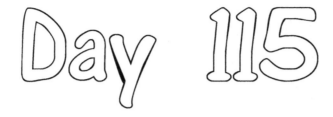

Day 115

Whatever you do, do your work heartily, as for the Lord rather than for men. Colossians 3:23.

_____

_____

_____

_____

_____

_____

_____

_____

festivals

Draw a picture of one of the festivals.

Day 116

But the disciples were indignant when they saw this, and said, "Why this waste?"

_____

_____

_____

_____

_____

_____

_____

_____

Color in today's vocabulary word. Draw a picture to show its meaning. It means to be angry, to show anger, to say something angrily. Here are some sentences that use the word.

He fumed when he found his tires had been slashed.

"I can't believe you did that!" he fumed.

Day 117

Being deeply grieved, they each one began to say to Him, "Surely not I, Lord?"

_____

_____

_____

_____

_____

_____

_____

Color in today's vocabulary word. Draw a picture to show its meaning. It means to bring danger on someone by revealing information, or to accidently reveal something hidden, or to hurt someone by breaking a trust.

Benedict Arnold betrayed his country.

Judas betrayed Jesus by leading soldiers to where they could arrest him.

Day 118

But Peter said to Him, "Even though all may fall away because of You, I will never fall away."

_____

_____

_____

_____

_____

_____

_____

Color in today's vocabulary word. Draw a picture to show its meaning. It means to be very determined to do something. Here are some sentences that use the word.

He was resolute about finishing before he went to bed.

Paul was resolute about going to Jerusalem.

Day 119

Then He said to them, "My soul is deeply grieved, to the point of death; remain here and keep watch with Me."

_____

_____

_____

_____

_____

_____

_____

Color in today's vocabulary word. Draw a picture to show its meaning. It means great happiness and excitement. Here are some sentences that use the word.

She was euphoric over her win.

They were euphoric on Christmas morning.

Day 120

Whether, then, you eat or drink or whatever you do, do all to the glory of God. 1 Corinthians 10:31

_____

_____

_____

_____

_____

_____

_____

_____

levers

Can you draw a lever or a weapon that uses a lever?

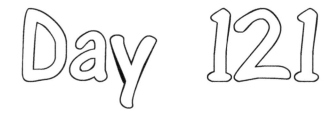

Day 121

But Peter was following Him at a distance as far as the courtyard of the high priest, and entered in, and sat down with the officers to see the outcome.

_____

_____

_____

_____

_____

_____

_____

legion

Color in today's vocabulary word. Draw a picture to show its meaning. It means a group of soldiers or a large group. Here are some sentences that use the word.

A legion was deployed to protect the area.

A legion of ants was marching into my home.

Day 122

The high priest stood up and said to Him, "Do You not answer? What is it that these men are testifying against You?"

_____

_____

_____

_____

_____

_____

_____

Color in today's vocabulary word. Draw a picture to show its meaning. It means to command or to urge. Here are some sentences that use the word.

I adjure you to keep this to yourself!

The king adjured his people not to panic.

Day 123

Then he began to curse and swear, "I do not know the man!" And immediately a rooster crowed.

_____

_____

_____

_____

_____

_____

_____

_____

Color in today's vocabulary word. Draw a picture to show its meaning. It means to discuss in order to make a decision. Here are some sentences that use the word.

We conferred and made plans to meet that afternoon.

It's wise to confer with your parents before making an important decision.

Day 124

Then Pilate said to Him, "Do You not hear how many things they testify against You?"

_____

_____

_____

_____

_____

_____

_____

Color in today's vocabulary word. Draw a picture to show its meaning. It means a person who can face hard things without showing that it's bothering them or not showing that something's bothering you. Here are some sentences that use the word.

A stoic in every sense of the word, the soldier refused to show his captors that he was upset in any way.

She was stoic when faced with her impossible decision.

Day 125

Greater love has no one than this, that one lay down his life for his friends. John 15:13

_____

_____

_____

_____

_____

_____

_____

_____

Al Capone

Can you draw a picture of how Al Capone finally got thrown in jail or how he used to win favor in communities?

Day 126

And all the people said, "His blood shall be on us and on our children!"

_____

_____

_____

_____

_____

_____

_____

scourge

Color in today's vocabulary word. Draw a picture to show its meaning. It means to whip or to cause pain and suffering, or a whip or someone or something that causes suffering. Here are some sentences that use the word.

The drought was a scourge on the farming community.

Jesus was scourged by the soldiers.

Day 127

At that time two robbers were crucified with Him, one on the right and one on the left.

_____

_____

_____

_____

_____

_____

_____

_____

Color in today's vocabulary word. Draw a picture to show its meaning. It means to support, to hold up, to accept. Here are some sentences that use the word.

Bear with me as I look for my keys.

I will bear the responsibility of making sure everyone gets there on time.

Day 128

Immediately one of them ran, and taking a sponge, he filled it with sour wine and put it on a reed, and gave Him a drink.

_____

_____

_____

_____

_____

_____

_____

_____

Color in today's vocabulary word. Draw a picture to show its meaning. It means to mock, to insult, to scoff, to taunt. Here are some sentences that use the word.

My wilting plants derided my efforts to develop a green thumb.

The soldiers derided Jesus.

Day 129

And Jesus cried out again with a loud voice, and yielded up His spirit.

_____

_____

_____

_____

_____

_____

_____

_____

precocious

Color in today's vocabulary word. Draw a picture to show its meaning. It means developing early, especially children who develop abilities early. Here are some sentences that use the word.

The precocious child had an impressive vocabulary.

The precocious plants peeked out before spring.

Day 130

Dear children, let us not love with words or speech but with actions and in truth. 1 John 3:18

_____

_____

_____

_____

_____

_____

_____

_____

resurrection

Draw a picture of the empty tomb or Jesus appearing to people after He was raised from the dead or of the apostles telling people about Jesus because they knew the truth.

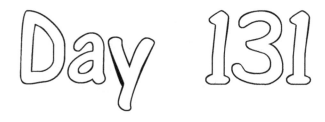

Fancy Font

Write your spelling words in a fancy font. You could write with bubble letters or make your own style. You should write at least five words.

comparable, drowsy, trimmed, instead, entrusted, ability, manner, master's money, afraid, weeping, category, cohesion, glorious, prison, least, extent

Day 132

Word Search

Find the words in the puzzle. Words are forwards, backwards, up, and down.

earthquakes, whoever, nursing, unless, anyone

vultures, tender, giving, grinding, experience

```
U  E  R  Z  W  G  N  I  S  R  U  N
T  X  E  B  O  T  E  N  D  E  R  N
G  P  A  J  Y  Y  O  S  B  G  U  J
U  E  R  U  H  A  V  I  A  N  W  B
E  R  T  G  R  I  N  D  I  N  G  J
N  I  H  M  U  I  M  O  I  C  F  R
W  E  Q  W  H  O  E  V  E  R  U  K
V  N  U  M  Y  G  X  P  Y  F  O  K
P  C  A  E  N  O  Y  N  A  W  G  D
Y  E  K  S  V  U  L  T  U  R  E  S
V  M  E  G  W  M  G  I  V  I  N  G
S  S  S  E  L  N  U  Z  K  F  B  Q
```

Day 133

Play Freeze Tag or Dungeon Escape

Here are the words you'll be playing with.

riot, starting, crucified, soldiers, garments,

abuse, rebuild, suspicious, ninth, sponge, sour,

whether, veil, frightened, saints, precocious

I Spy

Play I Spy! Cross out any word that could <u>not</u> be correct.
The vowels are: A E I O U.

Round one:

drew	perish	prophesy	crows	deserves
tore	silent	governor	testify	accused

Round two:

curse	prophesy	disposal	silent	deserves
drew	crows	accused	testify	treasury

Round three:

drew	perish	disposal	crows	prophesy
curse	silent	governor	testify	treasury

Round four:

drew	perish	disposal	crows	deserves
curse	silent	courtyard	testify	treasury

Fill in the Blank

Fill in the blanks with the letter pairs provided.

OO   EA   OU   AY   OU

w____k

p____red

M____nt of Olives

pr____ed

r____ster

Day 136

Fill in the Blank

Fill in the blanks with the letter or letters that would make the words plural.
Plural means more than one, for instance one bike, but two bikes.

toy   toy__

man   m__n

woman   wom__n

bike   bike__

child   child__ __ __

wish   wish__ __

goose   g__ __ se

deer   deer

Day 137

Who's the Winner?

Come up with a sentence or circumstance where one word wins out over the other. The man was <u>stoic</u> as the <u>legion</u> carried him off. The word legion wins because the legion carried away the stoic man.

Round 1: Which word is the winner?

tribulation: pain and suffering or the cause of pain and suffering

desolation: complete emptiness of a place or a heart or the destruction of a place so completely that it becomes empty because it is uninhabitable

Round 2: Which word is the winner?

elect: chosen person or people

callous: uncaring, rough and tough

Round 3: Which word is the winner?

prudent: making decisions carefully and wisely

inept: having no skill, clumsy

Day 138

Silly Sentences

Come up with four subjects and four predicates. Pair your subjects up with someone else's predicates and your predicates with someone else's subjects.

Example of subject: ball or The big red bouncy ball
Example of predicate: swims or swims across the Atlantic Ocean

Subjects:

_____

_____

_____

_____

Predicates:

_____

_____

_____

_____

Day 139

Matching

Match the words with their definitions. Write the numbers in the blanks.

1. abundance or an excessive amount, more than needed
2. to be angry, to show anger, to say something angrily
3. very determined to do something
4. great happiness and excitement
5. to support, to hold up, to accept
6. to mock, to insult, to scoff, to taunt
7. developing early, especially children who develop abilities early

_____ deride

_____ fume

_____ euphoric

_____ plethora

_____ precocious

_____ resolute

_____ bear

Day 140

Make it a sentence.

Add ending punctuation to make it a sentence.

How are you doing

I love this one

I can't wait

Yes, it is

Dogs are my favorite kind of pet

Do you think so

Are we there yet

No way

I'll be finished soon

If you ever find a mistake in one of our books,
please contact us through our site, genesiscurriculum.com.

Thank you for using the Genesis Curriculum.

Look for more years of the Genesis Curriculum using both Old and New Testament books of the Bible. Find us online at genesiscurriculum.com to read more about the latest developments in this expanding curriculum.

Genesis Curriculum also offers:

GC Steps: This is GC's preschool and kindergarten curriculum. There are three years (ages three through six) where kids will learn to read and write as well as develop beginning math skills.

A Mind for Math: This is GC's learning-together math for elementary students based on the curriculum's daily Bible reading. Children work together as well as have their own leveled workbook.

Rainbow Readers: These are leveled reading books. They each have a unique dictionary with the included words underlined in the text. They are also updated to use modern American spelling.

Made in the USA
Columbia, SC
21 November 2018